Saint Michael's

Reflections on a Journey

Saint Michael's
Reflections on a Journey

Copyright © Harrogate District Hospice Care Ltd
First published in 2011 on behalf of Saint Michael's by Scotforth Books
(www.scotforthbooks.com)

ISBN   978-1-904244-75-2
Typesetting and design by Carnegie Publishing, Lancaster.
Printed in the UK by Henry Ling Ltd, Dorchester

This book is dedicated to the people of Harrogate, Knaresborough, Ripon, Wetherby, Pateley Bridge and outlying communities.

Without your dedicated support over the past 25 years, Saint Michael's would never have come to be. We remain answerable to the communities we serve.

Saint Michael's is *your* hospice.

Thank you for the passion and belief shown by so many for so long...

Contents

Prologue	1
Beginnings	5
A short history of hospices in Britain	11
The Convent	19
The Crimple House Appeal	27
The story of Crimple House	35
Development of services	43
Fundraising through the years	71
Shops	93
Volunteers at Saint Michael's	105
The 'Saint Michael's Effect'	111

Foreword

When the idea of this book was first revealed we almost drowned under the deluge of stories, photos and memories of Saint Michael's. A huge amount of work has been enthusiastically invested into this project and yet the finished book is in some ways incomplete.

For every story captured in print there are probably forty or fifty that have escaped. The meaning and impact of Saint Michael's creates thousands and thousands of stories each day, out there among the communities that we serve. Most importantly stories from patients and relatives, but also from the remarkable number of volunteers who support, drive and motivate the constant journey of Saint Michael's. Add to these our wonderful and committed staff and those who have watched and witnessed the growth of this vital resource and then we begin to get a picture of just how many stories there must be, each one as individual as the care we provide for each patient. As we reach the 25 year mark it is inevitable that some of these stories will become lost, so however inadequate, we wanted to try and record at least a few.

This book does not represent the end of a journey – it is simply a milestone along the journey's path. Whatever each individual story tells us it is the collective of all the stories that best expresses the dynamic of Saint Michael's – constantly changing, growing and reacting to the needs of the community.

Saint Michael's journey goes on, but the parts played by so many dedicated individuals over the last 25 years will never be forgotten.

Thank you for your support.

Tony Collins
Chief Executive (2007 – Present)

Thanks and Acknowledgements

Thank you to all who contributed their memories, stories and photographs to this project. Your memories are important and precious and we are grateful that you took the time to share them. Thank you to Melanie Devine for your valuable advice and the many hours you gave to the project. Andrew Snow, thank you for the invaluable archive you created ensuring Saint Michael's history is preserved, not just to the benefit of this project but for many years to come. Thank you to Mike Landy for the many hours of editing you contributed and for your valuable advice. Hannah Webster, thank you for your encouragement, advice and practical support. Thank you Muriel Little and Cynthia Stevenson for your contributions and attention to detail. And thank you to all who have played a part in Saint Michael's journey over the last 25 years: without you we would not have had a story to tell.

Prologue...

In May 2010 we placed an open invitation in our newsletter and in local papers asking for memories and stories relating to the history of Saint Michael's. The response was overwhelming. The following letter describes one such memory…

Dear Sir/Madam,

I have just received the Saint Michael's magazine and read about the Voices of History project. I thought I'd write to tell you what I remember of the beginning as my sister, Mrs Catherine Morley was, I believe, the first patient.

First a little bit of the background. My sister was diagnosed with a deep brain tumour at the end of September 1978 at the age of 32. Her only child had been born earlier that same year. She at the time lived in Barton-in-Humber and had radio and chemotherapy in Hull. She survived the treatment and returned home with a lot of support from mum, good friends and neighbours. She was at first given 3 months to live, then 1 year, then 3 years.

Over the next 11 years Catherine defied the odds and her only treatment was yearly check-ups. In August 1989 mum took Catherine and Daniel on holiday to the south coast only to have Catherine taken to hospital in a coma. She was transferred to Wheatfields Hospice, as the hospital staff felt they could do no more for her. They were amazing at Wheatfields, and got Catherine back on her feet and able to go home to mum's.

During this time Saint Michael's was being opened and so Catherine was given a bed over a weekend to give mum some respite. Then she started going in for a week and only going home for weekends. The staff always said to mum that if she found it difficult at any time, just to let them know and a bed would be found for Catherine.

At one time Catherine was asked if everything was okay and she replied that a vacuum cleaner being used was rather noisy so they changed it for a quieter model! She was asked many times what she would like for her meals and it was always forthcoming, however difficult the task, nothing was too much trouble, the patients were put first at all times.

Catherine went in to Saint Michael's for the last time in the middle of December 1989, where she died peacefully on January 11th 1990, aged 43. The whole approach of nursing and caring was, and still is amazing. During the year of 1990 I would go across to Harrogate and pick up mum and take her to the coffee evenings which were held once a month for those bereaved to chat if they wanted to and also to raise a little money by having raffles.

I remember having great conversations with the Sisters from the Convent who would call in from time to time. These informal meetings were a godsend to us and many others who attended; just knowing you weren't alone after your loss. Mum is now in a nursing home, in her 96th year, has seen Daniel through his school years and supported him in gaining a 2:1 degree at University. He is now settled and happily married. Both mum and I still support the wonderful work of Saint Michael's; long may it continue.

Yours faithfully,

Judith Jackson

Beginnings...

In 1977 a group of six supporters of Wheatfields Hospice in Leeds sat down to the daunting task of penning five hundred individually addressed letters by hand. All residing in Harrogate, they wanted to bring the Leeds hospice to the attention of their local area. These letters were sent out to district nurses, GPs, Clergy and Churches throughout the Harrogate area.

The letters resulted in a hundred members of the local community coming together to listen to an address by a GP and a Social Worker, explaining just what exactly a hospice was. From this meeting a Harrogate fundraising group was born, and their first fundraising event, a coffee morning in 1977, raised £47. At this time, all efforts were concentrated on supporting Wheatfields. Harrogate had no dedicated palliative care services and although patients from Harrogate and its outlying areas were welcome at Leeds, many relatives had no means of transport and some patients felt uncomfortable travelling so far from home at a time in their lives already filled with uncertainty and fear.

Muriel Little, a member of the original support group, explains how the fundraising they carried out for Wheatfields Hospice, led to the beginnings of a dedicated Palliative Care service in the Harrogate area:

> "Posters for coffee mornings and jumble sales included my phone number as a reference point for further information, but people who rang were also asking how they could access the services in Leeds. Even some GPs rang to ask, so the support group began to consider that there was a local need, not necessarily for a hospice but for some form of palliative care service."

Members of Wheatfields Hospice Harrogate Support group presenting a cheque to a representative of Wheatfields Hospice in 1977 (L-R Muriel Little, Ros Jenkins, Diana Hinings)

Ursula Darley, who was to become the first nursing sister at Saint Michael's, also recognised the ongoing need for developing end of life care services:

> "I worked on the medical ward in Harrogate hospital, in haematology, so I used to see patients who were receiving their diagnosis. After rounds, the consultants would tell us that someone was 'a bit upset' – they really were not very good at giving bad news and there was no time to talk to families about what to expect. There was a big hole in the way cancer was treated in those days, and when patients came in for chemotherapy we became attached to them. I worked closely with the first Macmillan nurse in the area and I went on a 'Care for the Dying' course at St Gemmas Hospice in Leeds. It really brought home to me that with the re-organisation of the NHS there was a gap in our services to patients."

In 1985 the Harrogate support group brought together a steering committee made up of health professionals. One of their first acts was the naming of the organisation. In keeping with the majority of hospices already in existence, the group knew they wanted to use the name of a Saint. Meeting in September, they were inspired by Michaelmas celebrations honouring Saint Michael the Archangel, and so *Saint Michael's* was born.

The need for a hospice in Harrogate may have been clear to the members of the steering group but it did not meet universal support.

Dr Bob Jones had come to Harrogate as a GP in 1978, he remembers a mixed reaction from local GPs:

> To start with GPs in Harrogate weren't really sure how a hospice would work. We had questions such as who would be responsible for looking after the patients and would there be a doctor there the whole time? Very soon however we welcomed it with open arms. It became a wonderful refuge for our patients as the nursing care was first rate and patient care and comfort was the priority."

The group remained positive and determined and their clear vision and determination is the foundation upon which Saint Michael's was built. Many of the original Harrogate Support Group remain involved in the organisation to this day. Their contributions will never be forgotten.

The current version (2011)

The original design (1986)

From Daisy to Dolly

Just as the feast of Saint Michael (Michaelmas) was the inspiration behind Saint Michael's name, the daisy logo was inspired by the associated flower: the Michaelmas daisy.

The actual design was the winning entry in a small competition held in 1985.

The logo has changed a little over the years but is still easily recognisable and unmistakably synonymous with Saint Michael's.

The Michaelmas Daisy, also known as 'King George'. Its Latin name is Aster Amellus derived from the Greek 'Aster' (star) and 'Mella' (the River in Italy where it was first recorded)

A version from 2002

The daisy logo was even developed into a mascot, Dolly Daisy, who attended many fundraising events between 2003 and 2007, when she officially went into retirement!

Dolly was available for fundraising events throughout the community – here she is attending an event for Saint Michael's 'Yellow Week' campaign in 2004

Staff at Saint Michael's meet Dolly for the first time at her launch in 2003

In 2004, Dolly Daisy was immortalised as a soft doll. Sold for £2.50 each, they proved popular stocking fillers that year

A Short History of Hospices in Britain

[Hospice: house of rest for travellers; home for the destitute or (esp. terminally) ill.]

Concise Oxford Dictionary

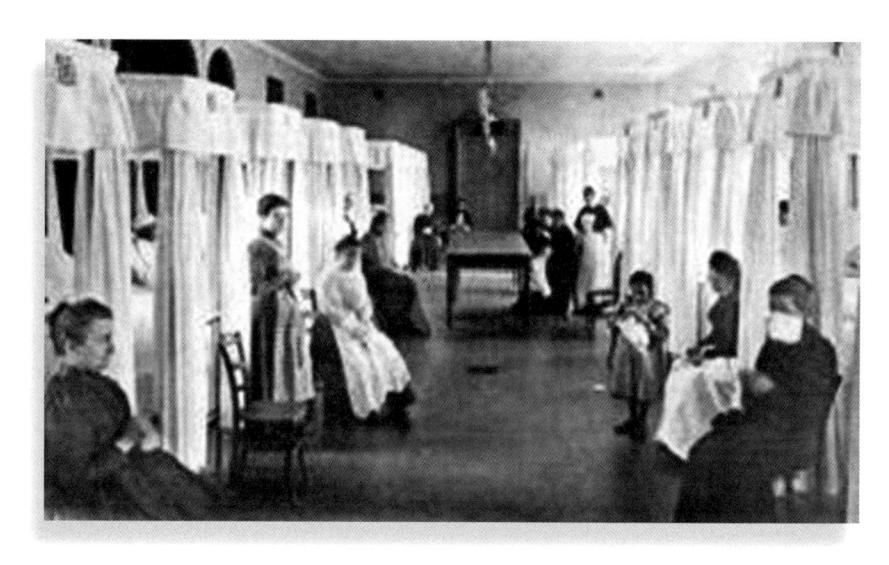

Dormitory of the Hospice of the Ladies of Calvary at Marseilles
(From an old postcard)

The very earliest hospices were opened by monasteries in Europe, *c.*1200. They provided rest, shelter and food for travellers. Those who were ill were cared for until they were well enough to continue their journey.

That tradition continued in this country, but after the Reformation, which saw the closure of many monasteries, convents and priories, those that remained became refuges for travellers and almshouses for the elderly.

By the nineteenth century the few remaining hospices offered an alternative to 'charitable hospitals for incurables' and workhouses. These were meant to care for the sick and destitute, but were dreaded by the very people they were supposed to help.

The word 'hospice' as a description of a place which cared solely for the dying was first used in 1842, when a 23-year-old widow, Jeanne Garnier, founded the Ladies of Calvary in Lyons, France.

Similar work was begun in 1879 by the Sisters of Mercy in Ireland, and was followed in mainland Britain in 1885 at what is now called Saint Columba's Hospice in Edinburgh.

Six years later came an important development for the hospice movement. The Hoare banking family appealed for funds 'to found a home for persons in an advanced stage of a mortal illness'. This resulted in the establishment of the Hostel of God in Clapham (now Trinity Hospice), staffed by the Sisters of St Margaret. It thus inaugurated the principle of heavy reliance on charitable donation, which continues to this day.

In 1892 the West London Mission under Dr Barrett opened St Luke's Home (later Hospital) for the Dying Poor, the first time a member of the medical profession had founded such a place.

The special requirements of cancer patients were soon recognised, and in 1911 Douglas Macmillan, having watched the suffering of his dying father, founded the National Society for Cancer Relief, now known as Macmillan Cancer Relief. It recognised the need for special homes and home care services to help those with advanced cancer.

Douglas Macmillan MBE (1884-1969)

In 1978 the 10th Macmillan nurse was appointed, the 1,000th in 1993. The 2,000th was funded in 2000.

The Macmillan National Institute of Education (MNIE), with 10 lecturers for training specialist cancer care professionals, was opened in 1998.

In 1948 Squadron-Leader Bernard Robinson, inspired by Winston Churchill's comment that casualties from cancer were far worse than those suffered in the Second World War, gathered together a group of like-minded friends and formed the Marie Curie Memorial Foundation, named after the lady who devoted her life to research into radiation and its use in cancer therapy.

Cicely Saunders

Widely regarded as the founder of the modern hospice movement, Dame Cicely Saunders was the leading figure in the campaign to establish hospices around the world.

Dame Cicely was educated at Roedean (1932–37) and St Anne's College Oxford (1938–1939 and 1944–45). She trained as a nurse at St Thomas's Hospital Nightingale School of Nursing from 1940–44; qualified AIMSW (Medical Social Worker) in 1947 and trained as a doctor at St Thomas's Hospital Medical School (1951–57) qualifying MB, BSc with Honours in surgery.

As Medical Officer of St Joseph's Hospice in Hackney, East London, she began to develop techniques of pain control. She established that it was possible to achieve better control by giving analgesic drugs at regular intervals *before* it became evident that the patient needed them. This not only alleviated pain but also, importantly, reduced the accompanying anxiety. Although other forms of cancer treatment have subsequently been developed, it is the regular administration of pain-killing drugs and personalised care of patients and support for their relatives which have become the hallmark of hospice palliative care.

Dame Cicely Saunders (1918–2005)

Cicely Saunders and St Christopher's

In 1948, while working as a volunteer nurse, she had fallen in love with a patient, a Polish waiter, David Tasma, who had escaped from the Warsaw Ghetto and was now dying of cancer.

He left her £500 to found a hospice, and 19 years later she was able to open St Christopher's at Sydenham in south-east London as the first research and teaching hospice.

St Christopher's soon became recognised as the international pioneer in the field of hospice practice, and Dame Cicely as the widely acknowledged founder and leader of the modern hospice movement. (She has always said that her patients – in both their needs and their achievements – were the real founders.)

It was under her direction that hospice work was extended to home care in 1969. Dame Cicely's work was widely acclaimed – she was the first person in nearly a century to receive an honorary doctorate of medicine, from the Archbishop of Canterbury, and in 1989 joined a handful of women to be awarded the Order of Merit.

She had already been made a Dame in 1980, the same year she was married to another Polish man to have a great influence on her life, artist Professor Marian Bohusz-Szyszko, who died in 1995.

St Christopher's: the world's first purpose-built hospice

Dr Saunders' Philosophy

"You matter because you are you, and you matter to the last moment of your life."

In 2001 Dame Cicely was awarded the world's largest humanitarian award – the Conrad N Hilton Humanitarian Prize of one million dollars – for her life's work caring for the dying.

She claimed to be guided by her Christian faith, strongly opposed euthanasia, and had a clear view of the role of hospices.

> She said, "I once asked a man who knew he was dying what he needed above all in those who were caring for him. He said, 'For someone to look as if they are trying to understand me.' Indeed, it is impossible to understand fully another person, but I never forgot that he did not ask for success but only that someone should care enough to try."

She saw dying as an opportunity to say 'thank you' and 'sorry' to family and friends. Her belief that dying is a phenomenon 'as natural as being born' was at the heart of a philosophy that sees death as a process that should be life-affirming and free of pain.

Today there are about 220 hospices in the United Kingdom and more than 8,000 in operation around the world.

Each year, about 60,000 people are admitted to hospices in the UK, with nearly half returning home again, and some 120,000 patients living at home are supported by hospice care, more than half of those dying from cancer.

Dame Cicely's work was instrumental in changing society's attitude to what had been regarded as the Western world's last taboo.

As she said: 'You matter because you are you, and you matter to the last moment of your life.'

> Dame Cicely Saunders died peacefully on Thursday 14 July 2005 at St Christopher's Hospice.

The Convent

In 1986, members of the newly named 'Saint Michael's Hospice Care' knocked on the door of the Convent of the Holy Child Jesus in Harrogate and asked the nuns if they could provide any accommodation to the group, however small. The nuns were keen to support Saint Michael's and offered the use of a small room with a desk and telephone. From this room the first of Saint Michael's services was launched: a cancer support telephone service. The nuns also agreed to the use of a larger room for a monthly drop-in service for patients and carers to receive information and support.

The Convent of the Holy Child Jesus, Oatlands Drive, Harrogate, 1986

PortaKabins are lowered into place in the grounds of the convent. These housed the hospice office, kitchen and staff quarters

ST. MICHAEL'S
Harrogate District
Hospice Care

CANCER HELP LINE
TEL. HARROGATE 880783
Operates every Thursday 2-4 p.m. and 6.30-8.30 p.m.
The Drop-in Centre is also open at St. Michael's Centre, The Convent, Oatlands Drive 2-4 p.m. Every Thursday
First and third Thursday of each month coffee served 10.30 a.m.-12 noon
Everyone welcome

Advertisement in the Harrogate Advertiser, October 1986

The newly built inpatient unit, nurses station and kitchen. The centre photo features Pauline Wiggins, HouseKeeper/Volunteer-Organiser and Jane Ranson, Matron

In 1988, after a substantial fundraising drive, work began to expand Saint Michael's services by creating inpatient rooms within the convent.

In 1989 the developments were complete and Saint Michael's opened a small inpatient unit. Five patient rooms were developed in the top corridor, space that had previously been used as the convent infirmary.

Ursula Darley applied to be a nursing sister at the hospice shortly before the opening of the inpatient rooms. She recalls a combination of excitement and trepidation during the very early days of Saint Michael's inpatient care:

> "When we opened, there were the two of us, with four staff nurses and care assistants – we were not all trained as hospice staff, but everyone went on courses at St Gemma's Hospice in Leeds and St Luke's in Sheffield. At that time there was a Nursing Home Inspection Team with the rules that the staff to patient ratio should be 1½ nurses to each patient, which was very different from the NHS. Moving from the NHS was very exciting, but it seemed like a pilot scheme, and so it was also a bit scary – we felt rather exposed, as there was nobody to ask, so we used our own best judgment to make decisions – it was a case of 'If it feels right, just do it'".

Karen (second from left) pictured with members of the nursing team after the move to Crimple House

Happy Memories

Karen Tremble began working as a Health Care Assistant at the Convent in November 1991 and has continued to work for Saint Michael's to the present day.

> "My first impressions of Saint Michael's at the Convent, were that the atmosphere was so peaceful, that there was lots of laughter and that it was not a depressing place at all. All the patients had their own rooms, and that was great because they had time and space to be together with their families, and even for their pets to visit.
>
> "We were very aware of the Catholic nature of the Convent, but we were always open to anyone. Having said that, many patients do go through a period of either wanting to talk to someone about their beliefs, or the opposite, they turn away from religion. Sister Margaret used to see all the patients every day, and ask them if they wanted to say prayers or mass, but she was very gentle about it, and she used to pray for them all anyway.
>
> "We had five beds for in-patients and outreach work which was mostly to do with symptom control. One nice thing was when we set the table in the lounge for the patient and their partner so they could have lunch together, just like at home.
>
> "Baths, either bed baths or a real bath, were quite a feature at Oatlands. Many of the patients were so thrilled to have a bath at all – lots of them couldn't manage at home, with climbing in and out, but we had a hoist. In the mornings, we used to help them get

dressed if they wanted to, then help them with their mouth care, apply cream to hands, legs and feet, do their hair for them, and for the ladies we used to help them with make-up and perfume. Anything to make them feel presentable for their visitors.

"At meal times we helped to serve and clear away, but we also helped patients to eat if it was difficult for them. If I was on lates, I had to cook the evening meals – I was absolutely traumatised by that – the pressure of cooking for someone else and to take the trouble to make it look as attractive and appetising as possible."

Sister Margaret Leonard was instrumental to the early success of Saint Michael's. It was under her guidance that Saint Michael's was granted permission to use the Convent building and facilities but her support extended much beyond this practical assistance. At the Convent, Sister Margaret visited each patient every day. Indeed she continued visiting long after Saint Michael's had relocated to Crimple House. Up until her retirement in 2000, Sister Margaret was an active supporter of Saint Michael's, providing pastoral support to staff and patients and helping fundraising efforts.

Karen remembers Sister Margaret's involvement at the Convent:

"Sister Margaret was an unbelievable help to us all. She was very gentle, and very quietly spoken. In fact, she was so quiet that she would come upstairs and I would turn round to find her right behind me! She was a trained nurse and she was also very fond of her sheep – they used to escape from time to time and we got calls from all the local houses. The relationship between the Convent staff and the Hospice staff was very good."

Sister Margaret Leonard remained a dedicated supporter long after Saint Michael's relocated to Crimple House. Here she is seen with Graham Archer, Chief Executive, in 2004

Search for a New Home

Saint Michael's time at the Convent on Oatlands Drive, Harrogate, was always intended as a temporary arrangement. The lease had been agreed for four years so there was plenty of time to look for suitable premises elsewhere.

Dennis Holman became Company Secretary of Saint Michael's in 1989 and he began almost immediately searching for an alternative home for the organisation. Many locations were considered, including a number of nursing homes. The administrators of the Convent remained keen to support Saint Michael's and suggested a building in the grounds of the Convent might be suitable. Dennis travelled to London to discuss this option but it was eventually decided that the site was not suitable for a number of reasons, particularly a lack of access.

In 1991 Dennis Holman became aware that the Crimple Estate, owned by ICI, had come onto the open market: an impressive 10.9 acres of land with three buildings. While this was a little too ambitious for Saint Michael's, Dennis kept a close eye on the estate and, after learning that the Home Owners Friendly Society (HOFS) were interested in the site, made an approach to them. An arrangement was made whereby the HOFS would purchase the entire estate and then sell Crimple House and 5 acres of land to Saint Michael's.

This marked the beginning of a wonderfully supportive relationship between Saint Michael's and the HOFS, which exists to this day. The two organisations continue to share the same grounds and HOFS (now commonly referred to as Engage Mutual Assurance), support Saint Michael's in many ways, including fundraising, volunteering and generous donations. The most famous is their sponsorship of one of Saint Michael's biggest fundraising events: the 'Engage Mutual Midnight Walk'.

Dennis Holman

Dennis Holman was the Company Secretary and Administrator at Saint Michael's between 1989 and 1992. It is widely accepted by those involved at this early stage that without Dennis' clear and ambitious vision of the future of the organisation, Saint Michael's may not have been set on the path to success that has seen it reach and surpass that early vision. Dennis Holman died in March 1992, having identified Crimple House as Saint Michael's future home and negotiated a purchase price. Sadly, he was unable to see these ambitions fulfilled.

Cynthia Stevenson, volunteer and chairman of the Board of Trustees at the time, pays tribute:

> "Dennis joined Harrogate District Hospice Care from a distinguished career in business. Among other things he was a graduate of Oxford University, a chartered accountant and a chartered secretary. As a volunteer, he assumed the roles of Company Secretary and Administrator. His input into the organisation was crucial to the management of the services at Oatlands Drive and to the transfer to Crimple House.
>
> "Dennis died in 1992, before the purchase of Crimple House was complete. His untimely death was a great loss to the organisation. Dennis was a 'hands on' person who would do anything to help patients and their relatives. This was much appreciated and he is remembered by many with respect and affection."

The Crimple House Appeal

Once the agreement had been made to purchase Crimple House there was the small matter of raising £1.4m to contend with. The agreed purchase price for Crimple House itself was £850,000, with additional money needed for adapting the building, organising the move between buildings, and of course maintaining the services that were already established.

The official launch of the Crimple House Appeal was held at Ripley Castle, through the kind support of Appeal President, Sir Thomas Ingleby, on 3rd June 1992

An official launch of the 'Crimple House Appeal' was held at Ripley Castle in the summer of 1992. Great emphasis was placed on garnering support from the communities of Harrogate and surrounding districts. Saint Michael's had been in existence at the Convent for three years and knowledge was increasing but there were still many people who did not know what the hospice did or who it was for. For this reason the Crimple House Appeal was not only about raising money, but also raising awareness.

One of the ways this was achieved was through a very close relationship between Saint Michael's and the local Ackrill Newspaper Group. David Marlow was a Saint Michael's fundraiser during the appeal years and he recalls how this strong relationship came about:

> "I went to see the editor of Ackrills and explained all about the organisation. They were keen to support us from the outset and agreed to feature Saint Michael's every single week, in some capacity. I used to attend a weekly meeting at Ackrill's offices to discuss what would go in that week's edition."

This support from the local newspaper company had a dramatic impact on Saint Michael's presence within the community. It also allowed the public to follow the progress of the appeal more closely, with regular updates as they neared their target, along with articles about the important work of Saint Michael's; a pertinent reminder of what all the hard work was for.

Advertisements in which ninety local companies declared their support for Saint Michael's appeared in the Harrogate Advertiser on Friday 29th October 1993. All money raised through the sale of advertisement space was donated by the Ackrill Newspaper Group to Saint Michael's – with the final figure reaching over £2500

Fundraiser David Marlow leads a march in support of Saint Michael's and to launch the sale of daisy pin badges, Harrogate Advertiser, November 5th 1993

By November 1992, just five months after being officially launched, Saint Michael's Crimple House Appeal had raised £300,000 towards the purchase of Crimple House. Support from the community was fantastic and events were being held within the community on almost a daily basis.

Throughout 1993 local support remained strong. In October of that year the fundraising effort was stepped up when 20,000 daisy pin badges were ordered, to be sold for £1 each. David Marlow, fundraiser at the time, recalls how the pin badge operation did not run as smoothly as it could have:

> "The badges were being delivered from China and we'd been given a promised delivery date. We had organised a launch event; a march through Harrogate, with much support and coverage from the local newspaper, for the week after their arrival. However, when, two days prior to the march date they still hadn't arrived, I started to get a bit concerned! There had been a delay getting them through customs and in the end we had to get a motorcycle courier to bring them up from London. They arrived on the morning of the march!"

Sales of the pin badge were excellent and within a few months a second order had been placed for a further 20,000.

By April 2004 the Crimple House Appeal had raised enough money to buy and prepare Crimple House. The appeal continued for a year afterwards and the full amount of £1.4 million was reached in March 1995.

Although the fundraisers at Saint Michael's were rightly proud of this incredible achievement they were careful not to celebrate too loudly. They now had a ten-bed inpatient unit and day care services to maintain and, with running costs of £500,000 a year, they did not want their supporters to think that the hard work was over. Saint Michael's has relied on support from local communities for twenty-five years and the Crimple House Appeal played an important part in forging and maintaining this crucial relationship.

The Big Move

On the 7th April 1994 Saint Michael's hospice moved from Oatlands Drive to Crimple House, Hornbeam Park. An open day was held on 12th April which was attended by over 300 people and on the 14th April the first inpatients were admitted.

Pauline Wiggins was the Housekeeper at Saint Michael's during the move. She remembers some of the practical considerations and echoes the feeling, described by many, of great sadness that Company Secretary Dennis Holman was not there to see it:

> "Oh, there was so much to do. We did take lots of equipment to Crimple, but we couldn't take the carpets and curtains, so they

The removal van arrives at the Convent to load up. After a five minute drive the van is ready to unload at Saint Michael's new home: Crimple House (over page)

The Crimple House Appeal

were sold. The kitchen was already fully fitted, because Crimple House had been used as the hospitality house for ICI. Oatlands had only had a family cooker and dishwasher! But because of the builders, our first job was to clean it completely, as it was covered in a thick layer of builders' dust! I was so proud to be part of the Hospice, and proud that Harrogate had raised the £1.4 million to do it. I was just so sad that Dennis was not there to see it open."

Ursula Darley, a nursing Sister during the time of the move, remembers the consideration given to patients' needs during the upheaval:

"When we moved to Crimple, we were anxious not to disrupt the patients, so some of them went into Harrogate Hospital, and we closed the admissions for a short time. It took a while to acclimatise and to find everything, but it was a fine building, especially for the in-patients."

An open day, held just five days after the move, was attended by three hundred local residents and allowed the community to see what all their support and hard work had achieved. It also offered some reassurances: both for those who were familiar with the Hospice at the Convent and those who had no experience of Saint Michael's or indeed any hospice. Karen Tremble, Health Care Assistant Manager at Saint Michael's explains:

> "I think the main thing is that people can be very wrong about what a hospice is for – and there is definitely a sense of peace, and even of magic, about Saint Michael's. When we were moving from Oatlands to Crimple we were concerned about whether the same feeling would still be there, but it is and it continues to be."

The Story of Crimple House

The land on which Crimple House stands has historically belonged to the township of Pannal, an ancient settlement owing its prosperity to the River Crimple which flows through it.

Pannal takes its name from Hugh Pagnell, granted land in the area by King Henry III in recognition of his services in the long Scottish Wars. Before that it was a part of the manor of Rosehurst, or Rossett, and appears in the Domesday book under that name.

Pannal School in 1915 (Photo courtesy of Anne Smith, Author of 'The History of Pannal')

Local history records that a family home stood on the present site in 1779. The first resident of Crimple House was John Bainbridge, who in 1789 was appointed a commissioner for the completion of the enclosure of Knaresborough Forest. His eldest son and heir, Captain John Bainbridge, founded Pannal School in 1817. On his death in 1856 he bequeathed it to trustees for the benefit of the parish.

In 1851 Oswald Milne, solicitor and magistrate, lived in Crimple House, and the 1861 census shows the house to be occupied by Thomas Simpson, Vicar of Pannal, and his family.

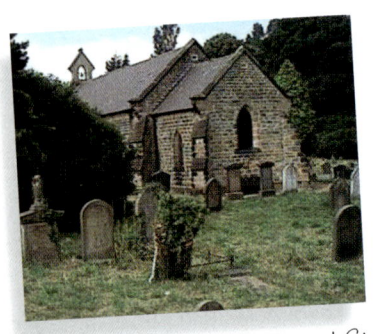

The 1871 census records the occupation of Crimple House by Charles Radcliffe, his wife Clementina, five children and eight servants. Charles was the son of Sir Joseph Radcliffe of Rudding Hall, Follifoot. The Radcliffe family held extensive lands in Pannal (formerly in the possession of the Bainbridges), on lease from the Duchy of Lancaster. In 1848 Sir Joseph granted part of Longlands Field and built St Joseph and St James' Church on trust for the Rector of Spofforth to provide services. Three chancel windows are in memory of Sir Joseph. In 1949 Captain Sir Everard Radcliffe gave land to form an extension to the churchyard on condition that a sixth of the land was to be used for Roman Catholic burials.

Church of St Joseph and St James, Follifoot

The house as it stands today was built in 1912 by William Whitehead, a mill owner from Bradford. He and his wife Lucy may have lived there part of the time: their two sons were born in the Bradford region in 1909 and 1914.

Robinson's Harrogate Directory, 1919, lists the occupant of Crimple House as J. H. McEwan. He commissioned the following drawing:

And above, how it looks today.

In 1848 the 31-arch Crimple Viaduct was completed. This carries trains on the Harrogate branch of the Leeds–York line. The original line from Leeds to Harrogate ran *under* the viaduct.

View of Crimple Viaduct from Crimple House

The Story of Crimple House

The viaduct certainly adds to the charm of the landscape around Crimple House.

The Radcliffes continued in residence at the house. According to the 1901 census William Manley lived there with his wife, Mary Filumina Radcliffe (daughter of Sir Joseph Radcliffe, 3rd Baronet), her brother Roger and a cousin, Charles Radcliffe. The Manleys were still there in 1911, with their only child, Mary Charlotte.

Crimple House – the present building

In 1955 ICI acquired the property and used it as a sort of private hotel and clubhouse for its staff from the nearby laboratories. It was in these labs that crimplene (named after Crimple Beck) was invented.

ICI continued at Crimple House until 1994, when Harrogate District Hospice Care Limited registered the building as a nursing home.

Crimple House today

Crimple House as a Hospice – adapting the building

For all its charm and beauty, Crimple House was never built to house a hospice service and considerable work has been carried out to adapt it.

In 2002 a fundraising appeal was launched to enable the building of an extension, the main aim of which was the creation of a new wing. The 'Keystone Appeal' as it was known set out to raise £500,000 and support from the community was immediate and substantial. The appeal raised £130,000 in less than six months, allowing building work to begin.

Saint Michael's employees pose with members of the building team

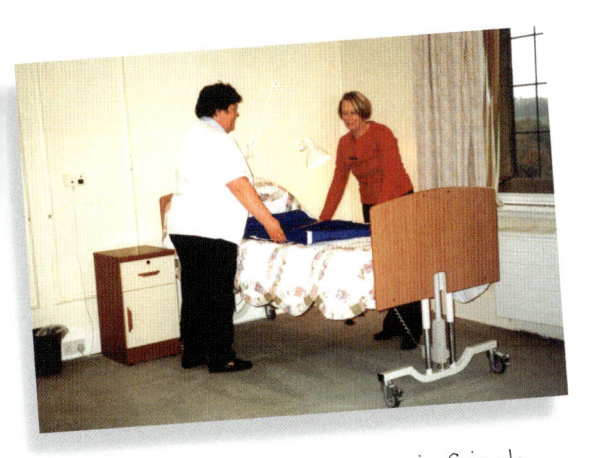

Above – an inpatient room in Crimple House, 2003

Below – an inpatient room in 2011, after the addition of an overhead tracking system, flat screen television and individually controlled air conditioning system.

Day Care benefited most from the development. The original ceilings and walls were in poor condition and these were replaced, along with the creation of bright, airy rooms and a separate quiet room, lounge and individual treatment rooms. The building development also allowed all inpatient rooms to become single occupancy and for general improvements such as superior nurse call and burglar alarms.

In 2002 the fundraising team was operating out of two Portakabins in the house grounds, due to lack of office space. The building plans took this into consideration and upon completion the team was welcomed in from the cold to newly created offices.

Crimple House seen here during and after the building of the Day Care wing

By spring 2003 the Keystone Appeal had reached its target and the building work was complete.

In 2009 the reception area of Crimple House was further developed to provide a lighter, brighter, more welcoming interior and in 2010 the inpatient unit was completely refurbished to ensure patients' needs were met with the most up-to-date equipment and facilities.

The new Day Care facilities were officially opened by Anne, Duchess of Norfolk, who was at the time Patron of the national charity 'Help the Hospices', 14th October 2003

Development of Services

While for many people the outward face of Saint Michael's within the community is that of fundraising and shops, for those involved in running the organisation, the core of the hospice's beliefs and ambitions has always been about getting things right for those who really matter – patients and their families.

After fourteen years as Saint Michael's Clinical Director, Ann Cairns has seen many changes in the clinical services offered. Despite many practical and necessary progressions within service provision, Ann notes that passion, drive, energy and enthusiasm have remained essential constants throughout the past 25 years and Saint Michael's is entrusted by the community to continue this mission on into the development of all future services.

> "We have seen many changes in the clinical services offered. The complexity of clinical care required to meet the range of end stage illnesses which patients are requiring our care and support with is now greatly expanded. Advances in medical treatment and interventions have vastly changed the extent of specialist palliative care provision at Saint Michael's. Intravenous infusions, use of respiratory support units, advances in wound care management, specialist 24 hour medical staff on call, specialist dietitian advice and guidance, nutritional analysis of patient menus, extensive equipment and monitoring is now required and forms part of our modern and forward thinking services. Patient accessibility to the

internet within inpatients and day therapy encourages different modes of communication and can be of great assistance to people with communication difficulties."

In twenty-five years Saint Michael's has grown from an information helpline into an organisation that supports over two thousand patients each year. In 2007 the leadership team, recognising the growing need for Saint Michael's services, wrote an ambitious strategy for further development. At its core was an over-arching aim to double the number of patients benefiting. This was achieved in 2011 and Saint Michael's continues to grow in response to the needs of those in the communities it serves.

The cost of making this happen each year has risen from £300,000 in 1992 to £3.9 million in 2011. In order to raise this amount and maintain service provision, the Saint Michael's team has grown from a handful of volunteers to more than a hundred members of staff and over six hundred volunteers.

The First Services

In 1986 Harrogate District Hospice Care Helpline was launched. This was Saint Michael's first direct service available to the people of Harrogate and surrounding districts and was primarily a support and information service, with a small amount of advice offered where appropriate. It was based in a small room within Saint Michael's first home; the Convent on Oatlands Drive, and was available all day on Thursdays. A small group of volunteers (pictured below) worked on a rota system answering calls and, at all times other than Thursdays, it was diverted to the home of founder volunteer Muriel Little. Within the first four months of the service being available, they had received one hundred and fifty four calls.

Also in 1986, a drop-in centre was made available, between 2pm and 4pm each Thursday, providing social contact and support for patients. Coffee mornings twice a month kept the public involved in the development of the charity and raised valuable funds.

At this time a professional Advisory Group was also formed, which included Health Authority members, Palliative Care consultants and General Practitioners and in August 1989, after a substantial fundraising drive, Saint Michael's opened its first Inpatient Unit.

A new Community Outreach scheme provided training for volunteers who were then able to offer relief to carers of patients in their own homes. This was further extended in 1990 thanks to the allocation of government funding, allowing the employment of nurses for night-sitting.

In 1993, Day Care facilities were available for the first time at Crimple House. A dedicated specialist Lymphoedema service followed in 1997. Bereavement support was always a part of the service provided by Saint Michael's and in 2009 this was formalised with the opening of *Just B*, the Saint Michael's community bereavement service.

Inpatient Unit

The opening of a 5 bed inpatient unit in 1989 was a great triumph for those who had fought tirelessly for years in order first of all to convince others that the service was needed, and secondly, raise the money to make it happen. Patients were referred to the service by their GP or specialist care worker and in a 1990 newsletter Saint Michael's printed a report on how the service was used during those first weeks:

> After the hospice has been open for 166 days, first with three beds and then five, these are the statistics:
> During this time the hospice has had 37 patients; 19 ladies and 18 men. Of these, four remain in our care, two have gone home after receiving respite care, and the others spent their last days with us. The average length of stay is 15 days and the bed occupancy is 77%. There can be no doubt of the need for the hospice care provided at Saint Michael's.

Patients were cared for by a small nursing team, supported by volunteers. Doctors were not employed directly by Saint Michael's until after the move to Crimple House. Bob Jones, a GP in Harrogate at the time explains:

"The GPs were responsible for their own patients, and so we were in and out on a regular basis – of course when it was at Oatlands there were only 5 in-patient beds. After Crimple House opened, it became apparent that there would be a need for a dedicated 'inhouse' doctor, to raise the status of the hospice and offer increased consistency in care received there. Jill Warren was appointed and from then the GPs left their patients in Jill's excellent care, although we would call in to see them and it was very much a partnership."

Dr Jill Warren joined Saint Michael's as Medical Director in 1996 and the multi-disciplinary team, responsible for the care of patients has continued to grow.

The team currently includes a dietitian, occupational therapist, physiotherapist, doctors, specialist care nurses, psychologist, social worker, chaplain, Motor Neurone Disease (MND) specialist, consultant in palliative medicine and a clinical nurse specialist (employed to work in the community).

Saint Michael's Multi-Disciplinary Team pictured in 2010

Saint Michael's nurses showing off one of the newly purchased hydraulic beds, bought with money raised by a patient's family combined with a fundraising drive by the 'Harrogate Citizen's Guild of Help' in 2001.

Improving Facilities and Equipment

Many advances have been made over the years, and refurbishments carried out, to ensure that the ten inpatient rooms are of the highest standard. Emphasis is placed upon maintaining dignity and independence.

Improved facilities extended to those available to the nursing team. An extension to their office in 2002 provided a little more breathing space!

Before and after photos of the improvements to the nurses' station in 2002.

Development of Services

Respite Care

Since the first inpatient beds were opened in 1989, Saint Michael's has offered respite care. In recent years one of the inpatient rooms has been set aside for this purpose only. Karen Tremble, Health Care Assistant Manager, explains the reasons behind offering respite care and the logistics required to make it successful.

> "People need respite care because of family commitments, or a change in drug regime, or just to give someone a break. It is agreed with all their home care team, and they are booked in for a specific time. Then when they leave, we inform the GP surgery, the district nurse and the ambulance, and of course the carers. We have a very good relationship with all the Health Care Professionals, and there are regular case conferences, often these include the social worker or the occupational therapist too, so that things are organised properly at home."

Pets as Therapy

In 2001 a couple of Labradors, Rupert and Henry, became regular visitors to the hospice as part of the 'Pets as Therapy' scheme. They offered a great deal of comfort to many patients and Saint Michael's has continued to welcome Pets as Therapy animals.

Ann Burrell (pictured right with Scrabble) has been a volunteer for six years and comes in with her dogs three or four afternoons a week. Domino and Scrabble are Leonbergers. These large dogs have a quiet, gentle nature, perfect for this work. Ann explains:

"I just sit and chat whilst the dogs go from patient to patient, accepting strokes, cuddles and attention, and offering comfort and unconditional love. Domino in particular is very receptive to people and seems to know who needs him most."

Day Therapy

Day Care was available at Saint Michael's, within the Convent, each Tuesday from 10am–3pm. Patients were referred to the service by their GP or specialist healthcare provider, just as they are today, and they spent the day socialising, playing cards, enjoying refreshments and a home cooked meal.

A qualified nurse, Kath Gill became a volunteer at Saint Michael's after her retirement in 1987. She helped in Day Care at the Convent and remembers her time spent there as 'fun', perhaps not a word one might think of when considering a hospice:

"I worked in Day Care from May 1990, and did some relief work. It was mainly nights, but I was available on call too. In Day Care the patients came in and had a cup of coffee, then later a very good home-cooked lunch – they could sit and chat, do a crossword, bring in their knitting, do some craft work – and all the time there were people to look after them so they felt comfortable and happy. In fact, I could say that Day Care was 'fun' – everyone thinks the Hospice is a dreary and sad place, but it isn't – it's a very happy place to work, and although the deaths are very sad, especially if they are young people, it is a very rewarding place. And while the patients are being cared for, their carers can go shopping, have a walk or a break, or meet their friends for coffee. Time out is very important for carers."

On the 17th August 1993 Day Care opened at Crimple House, the first of the services to move to the new building. It remained available on a Tuesday for a year until demand grew to such a level that a second day was introduced. Up to twelve patients could be accommodated each day and volunteer drivers were recruited to collect patients from their homes in the morning, bring them to the hospice, and then return them home at three o'clock. Demand for Day Therapy services continued to climb and in 1997 the service was extended to three days.

In 2003 after the expansion and refurbishment of Day Care facilities, increased treatment space meant that in addition to specialist nursing, complementary therapies, such as Indian Head Massage, Reflexology and Reiki could be introduced. Saint Michael's began recruiting skilled volunteers to carry out this service. Louise Booth was appointed Complementary Therapies Leader and, in an interview for Saint Michael's newsletter at the time, she explained the benefits of such therapies:

> "Life changes due to altered health can often be stressful. Distress can cause psycho-biological reactions such as palpitations, insomnia, fatigue, aggression, difficulty concentrating, headaches, loss of sense of humour and depressing thoughts. Complementary therapies can help a person to cope with their illness and any treatment by promotion of relaxation and feelings of well-being. Any complementary therapy treatment is offered within the context of conventional health care treatment at Saint Michael's and is part of the whole care plan devised for an individual patient."

A Complementary Therapist volunteer paints the nails of a patient during a visit to Saint Michael's Day Therapy service

In 2008 the Day Care service was extended once again and a fourth day offered. This formed part of the aims of the development strategy launched in 2007 and created space for an additional thirteen patients each week.

In 2010 Saint Michael's further developed the day therapy service, increasing the emphasis placed upon patients' individual needs and goals. Shelagh Outhwaite, Saint Michael's Head of Outpatient Services explains:

> "The Day Therapy service has become very much led by patients' needs and the goals they would like to achieve. Each patient is different but one example of this is a patient experiencing lots of anxiety. The appropriate members of the multi-disciplinary team (MDT) will work with that patient; in this case it might be the complementary therapy team and our occupational therapist. If a patient wants to improve mobility, our physiotherapist would provide a lot of support. It's very much a team effort however and the MDT meet regularly to discuss patients' progress and changing needs. We aim to discharge patients after ten weeks, after hopefully achieving the goals set out, however the day therapy service is always individual and tailored to different people's needs. When a patient is discharged we always make it very clear that we have a 'revolving door' and they can be referred back into the service."

Lymphoedema Clinic

In February 1997 funding became available to open a specialist lymphoedema support service, and the first patient was welcomed in September that same year.

Lymphoedema is a side effect of some cancers or can be hereditary. It is caused when the normal drainage system in the body is damaged or interrupted in some way. People living with this condition often get a painful swelling throughout their body, including their arms and legs. The service offered by Saint Michael's is the only specialist clinic in the area and therefore provides vital physical and psychological support for people while also working proactively to prevent the condition.

In recent years Saint Michael's Lymphoedema Clinics have been extended throughout local communities. By its very nature it can be a debilitating condition so emphasis has been placed upon making treatment available at a variety of locations. At present there are two clinics in Harrogate, as well as one in Ripon and one in Knaresborough.

Treatment includes specialist bandaging and massage and more recently, a unique form of group exercise called the Lebed Method.

In the Community

In 1989 Saint Michael's successfully opened a five-bed inpatient unit and it quickly became apparent that there was a growing need to support patients in their own homes, whether this be before, after or instead of accessing the inpatient unit service. The Community Outreach programme was launched when a group of volunteers were trained in providing support to patients within their own homes. Kath Gill was one such volunteer:

> "I attended the first meeting for 'Home Carers' which was held on 6 September 1990. When patients were discharged from the hospice after treatment or if they wanted to die at home, the outreach programme gave carers and families the chance to get some sleep or to pop out for an hour. I remember one chap whose wife was dying. He wouldn't go to sleep, just sat for hours and hours watching cine films – he was so frightened that his wife would die if he went to sleep."

The first family joined the Community Outreach scheme in December 1989 and over the next year more than fifty families were referred to the service. The training programme for volunteers was turned into an annual event, facilitated by volunteer and nursing tutor Cynthia Stevenson:

> "Each year, starting in September we trained a group of volunteers for the Community Outreach work. The training sessions ran on Thursday afternoons over a period of eight weeks. Although some volunteers were registered nurses, we welcomed help from volunteers with many different backgrounds."

Community Outreach continued with success for many years. In November 1992 its name was changed to Home Care, the term used by most other hospices at the time. Families' involvement with the service varied widely; some accessed support just once, others relied on the service for more than a year.

Although the Saint Michael's Home Care scheme came to an end in 2003, the commitment to enabling patients to make their own choices about the care they receive has never faltered. Tony Collins, Saint Michael's Chief Executive since 2007 explains:

> "Of our patients, around half die in the Hospice and half at home. We believe that we can enable people to make their own choice. Of course this means a lot of education is necessary, and we are establishing closer links with many of the nursing homes in the area, giving training to their staff, so we can work with them and their patients. This means that many of our staff are now out in the community, and we provide management for the local Macmillan nurses."

Bereavement support and Just 'B'

Grief is a normal and natural response to death and most people who experience it come through safely with the help of family and friends. Some people welcome additional support at this time and the hospice has always provided a variety of opportunities to receive this.

Since 1990 Saint Michael's has offered an opportunity for bereaved family members to meet once a month to support one another in a social setting. Initially held at the Convent, and then transferred to the large events room at Crimple House, these monthly coffee mornings have provided comfort and reassurance to many. Occasionally speakers were invited and Saint Michael's staff and volunteers were always in attendance.

Throughout the 90s this monthly bereavement support service was run in a quite formal way; the families of patients who had accessed Saint Michael's services were contacted by letter and invited to attend. Many of the hospice staff underwent extensive training in order to provide the service and it was estimated that between twelve and fifteen families accessed bereavement support each month.

The Just 'B' 'brand' is intentionally dissimilar to Saint Michael's easily recognisable daisy logo. This emphasises the significant distinctions between the bereavement service and other services offered by the organisation.

Saint Michael's Community Outreach volunteers also received bereavement support training in preparation for spending time with patients, carers and families within the community, as did staff and volunteers who supported patients and families within Day Care.

In 2007 it was recognised within the hospice that there was a need In Harrogate for greater bereavement support, not only for those affected by death through terminal illness, but for individuals bereaved by any means. This led to the development of Saint Michael's most recently launched service: a dedicated bereavement support service. The first, and so far only, Saint Michael's service that is available to children and young people as well as adults, it was given a name that would separate it from other Saint Michael's services: *Just 'B'*

Just 'B' was developed to offer different levels of support, depending on an individual's particular need. It may be that some written information, a leaflet or website, provides enough reassurance. For some a telephone call or one-off session will suffice. Others might attend a longer series of one to one or group support sessions. Saint Michael's also employs a psychologist who can offer advice and further help. Jane Driver, Head of Bereavement at Saint Michael's explains:

> "At Just 'B' we believe that with the right support, at the right time, children, young people and adults can find a way to manage their grief and embrace a future where they can live and remember their significant person in a healthy and positive way."

Remembering

Light up a Life

Saint Michael's first 'Light up a Life' event was held on Sunday 6th December 1998. Always taking place at this time of year, the event provides an important opportunity for families to remember loved ones in the run up to the Christmas period: an emotional time for many people, when feelings of loss are often heightened. If they wish, families can dedicate a light on the tree to their loved one and at the climax of the event, the lights are switched on. 'Light up a Life' also includes readings, music and an opportunity for quiet reflection and remembrance.

In 1999 two services were held: in addition to the Crimple House event, a tree was installed for Saint Michael's at Lightwater Valley theme park, near Ripon. In 2000 the event was expanded even further with three trees – Crimple House, Ripon Cathedral and Central Harrogate's Victoria Shopping Centre. Since 2001 two services have been held each year, at Crimple House and Ripon Cathedral, on the first and second Sunday in December.

Preparing the tree for the 2003 service at Crimple House

After the lights have been switched on during the 2003 event. The Crimple House event is held outside in the beautiful grounds

In addition to the outdoor Crimple House service, an annual Light up a Life event is held at Ripon Cathedral. Pictured is the service in 2003. Attendees hear readings and music, and take time to reflect and remember

60   saint michael's

Book of Remembrance

When Crimple House was extended in 2003, an important addition to facilities was a 'Room of Quiet'. A tranquil space, set aside for reflection and prayer, it is also the home of Saint Michael's Book of Remembrance. This leather bound journal holds the names of Saint Michael's former patients. At a family's request, their loved one's name is added to the book by a skilled volunteer calligrapher, and families are welcome to come back into Saint Michael's to see the entry and spend time in this peaceful room.

Thanksgiving Services

Since 1990, Saint Michael's has held a Thanksgiving Service each year. These services offer another opportunity for families and friends to remember loved ones. They also offer a chance for Saint Michael's staff, volunteers, patients, families of patients and the general public to give thanks for the work of the organisation and the significant achievements made possible through the support, determination and hard work of many. Held at Crimple House or at different churches within Harrogate and surrounding districts each year, these services also help to raise the charity's profile.

Saint Michael's Hospice
Invite you
to come and share in our
Thanksgiving Service
to remember
our loved ones and friends
Sunday 7 October
St. Andrew's Church
Starbeck, Harrogate
3.30pm
We look forward to seeing you there

SAINT MICHAEL'S HOSPICE ANNUAL
Thanksgiving Service
SUNDAY 1st OCTOBER 2006 AT 3.00PM
Please join us
At Saint Michael's Hospice, Crimple House,
Hornbeam Park Avenue,
Harrogate
For the work of the Hospice and
In Remembrance of our loved ones.
ALL WELCOME

From Saint Michael's newsletters: September 2006 (above) and September 2001 (left)

Spiritual Support

Despite its name, Saint Michael's has no religious affiliation and welcomes patients with any or no religious or spiritual outlook. However, Saint Michael's duty of care has always attended to the spiritual and religious needs of patients and their families. Muriel Little, founding volunteer, explains:

> "There was a chaplain from Day One, and all the churches in Harrogate were involved. Whilst we are completely non-denominational, and accept those who have no faith, it is important to many of the patients to have someone to talk to in confidence, to off-load their worries at the end of their lives."

Saint Michael's has benefited from a number of Chaplains over the years; each with their own approach. Saint Michael's current Chaplain, the Rev Jonathan Bower, gives his view on the role of a hospice Chaplain:

> "As Chaplain, I see my role as primarily one of 'spiritual companionship', accompanying people in their journey. Pastoral, spiritual and religious care are my priorities – I am available to those professing any faith as well as for those who have no particular faith. As Chaplain, I make space and time for people, offering compassion and care, and an opportunity to explore personal and spiritual issues that can come to the fore as the end of life approaches. It is a particularly precious gift to be able to journey alongside those who are nearing the end of life or facing end of life issues.

"I am increasingly conscious of entering a patient's room with nothing in my hands to ease pain, reduce sickness and heal wounds, but attempting to offer something that is not auditable, quantifiable or even visible. Yet many people know and see the effects of good spiritual care, sensitively and carefully offered, as spirits are soothed and a sense of worth and dignity is restored. This is not just the task of Chaplain, it is the task of the entire multidisciplinary team. It is an honour and a very humbling privilege to be part of that team at Saint Michael's."

The housekeeping and catering team in 2001

Behind the Scenes

It goes without saying that cleanliness and hygiene are paramount within any kind of clinical environment. At Saint Michael's the housekeeping teams have worked tirelessly over the years to maintain optimum good hygiene throughout the building and to meet strict infection control standards. In the early days of Saint Michael's it was a case of 'all hands on deck' and at particularly busy times volunteers were recruited to assist with the laundry (often 150 pieces each day).

Pauline Wiggins, Saint Michael's first housekeeper, remembers challenges encountered in the early days:

> "Originally there was only a tiny laundry room with a small washing machine and dryer. There were two volunteers from Marks and Spencers, and when Vera – the laundry volunteer – said there was too much laundry for that little room and couldn't we put it in the bigger room downstairs, M&S raised the money for a new washing machine."

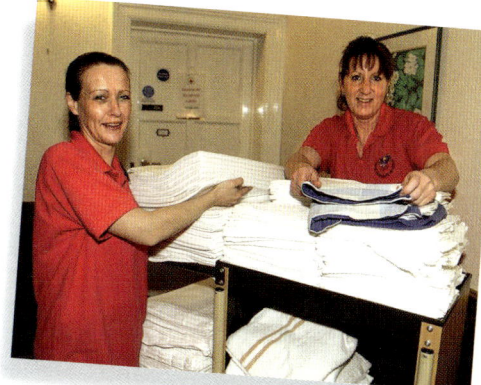

Members of the housekeeping team in 2005

Development of Services

In recent years the housekeeping team has expanded to meet the needs of the growing organisation. Helen Czupczyc, Saint Michael's Housekeeping Supervisor has worked at Saint Michael's for ten years:

"As the organisation has expanded, so have the demands on the housekeeping team (both at Crimple House and Burton House, where JustB is housed). More housekeepers are needed and we work closely with Kathy Newbould, head of Saint Michael's Inpatient Unit, in order to keep and maintain a very high level of cleanliness."

Members of Saint Michael's housekeeping team in 2011

Food Glorious Food

Since the first inpatient beds opened in 1989, Saint Michael's has recognised the importance of nutritious and appealing food, as this extract from the July 1990 newsletter shows:

> Many of our patients have quite good appetites when their symptoms have been controlled. We try to meet the needs of the patients by providing nutritious, well presented food at any hour of the day or night and to respond to what the patients fancy. We find that on the whole patients prefer straightforward simple food, but all tastes are catered for.

As Housekeeper, Pauline Wiggins was responsible for all aspects of catering during the first years of the inpatient unit:

"It was one of the things I had to learn about; the special diets that people have if they are very ill with cancer. Chemotherapy and drugs make people change their tastes; sometimes they can't bear the smell or taste of something, or they want to eat something really sweet, so we had to cater for each person as an individual. I went to St Gemma's Hospice in Leeds for some training about diets. They gave me a lot of insight into that, but also into how important it is to treat the relatives as much as the patients."

Members of Saint Michael's catering team in 2011 showing off a cake they created for a patient's special occasion

In recent years Saint Michael's has employed the services of a dietitian, and continues to focus on nutrition as an important aspect of overall care. As with all patient care, nutritional needs are individualised. Patients' needs vary with illness and its progress. Maintaining dignity is paramount and this is so with the provision of food. Wherever possible adaptations are made that allow patients to continue to feed themselves and to enjoy the experience of eating. This might include specially designed bowls that allow a patient to eat using only one hand, or very small portion sizes, which are often more appealing to a patient experiencing nausea.

Above all, pleasure and enjoyment are paramount, and every effort is made to ensure patients are able to continue to enjoy food.

Education and Raising Awareness

> **OATLANDS INFANT SCHOOL**
> HOOKSTONE ROAD
> HARROGATE
> NORTH YORKSHIRE
> HG2 8BT
> Tel: Harrogate (01423) 871036
> Fax: (01423) 874576
> email: oatlands @ lineone.net
> Mrs J E Davis : Headteacher
>
> Dear Ann,
> Thank you so much so coming to our Asembly. I realy injouyid it I liked your pichers you made our Asembaly realy intreshing!. When I grow up I am going to be a nures. I am shore it is going to be good fo~~r~~ fun at ~~se~~ St. Michaels hospice with lots of love Stephanie xxx
>
> "Excellence and quality are the hallmarks of this school" OFSTED 1995
> "The school successfully promotes high attainment... many lessons provide opportunities for spontaneous awe and delight" OFSTED 1999

Saint Michael's has always promoted its work through talks and presentations in the community.

This letter from 'Stephanie' to the hospice after a talk at Oatlands Infant School is a reflection of the value of such presentations and the enthusiasm with which they are received.

It is also crucial that the hospice collaborates with other health and social care providers to share expertise and specialist knowledge. From this commitment the Saint Michael's education programme was developed in 2008. Through improved staff training and increased understanding of end of life care issues, Saint Michael's is contributing to future developments within the field. Since 2008, 66 healthcare assistants and 30 GPs have received training from Saint Michael's specialists.

Fundraising Through the Years

As annual running costs rise, so of course must fundraising revenues. This chart shows how costs have soared since 1990:

1990

£320 thousand

1996

£0.5 million

2011

£3.9 million

And here is a breakdown of fundraising revenues for 2009–10:

LEGACIES	£896,067
RETAIL	£636,573
COMMUNITY SUPPORT	£515,821
CORPORATE SUPPORT & TRUSTS	£491,000
NHS	£440,579
EVENTS	£353,088
LOTTERY	£209,086
INVESTMENTS	£ 2,979

Support from the Community

There was no lack of effort when it came to fundraising in the early days of Saint Michael's, as these extracts from the March 1990 Newsletter show (all proceeds were to Saint Michael's):

7 March	Knaresborough Flag Day. Helpers needed.
17 March	Square Dance, Mechanics Institute, Kirkby Malzeard. £4.75 inc. supper.
7 April	Egg-stravaganza, Gilphay Village Hall. Coffee & stalls.
7 April	Harrogate Flag Day. Collectors needed.
14 April	Charity Fair, Pateley Bridge Memorial Hall.
15 April	Concert – Band & Choir from Finland & USA, Birstwith Church.
24 April	Fashion Show by 'Good Going' of Northallerton. Valley Gardens.
30 April	Savoury & Surprise Evening, Lonsdale House, Hampsthwaite. £2.50.
18 May	May Ball, Rudding Park. Tickets £35.
26 May	Coffee Morning, Pateley Bridge Memorial Hall.
3 June	Clay Pigeon Shoot.
30 June	Garden Party, 35 Oatlands Drive.
14 July	Social Evening, Walden, Station Lane, Hampsthwaite. Tickets £2.50.

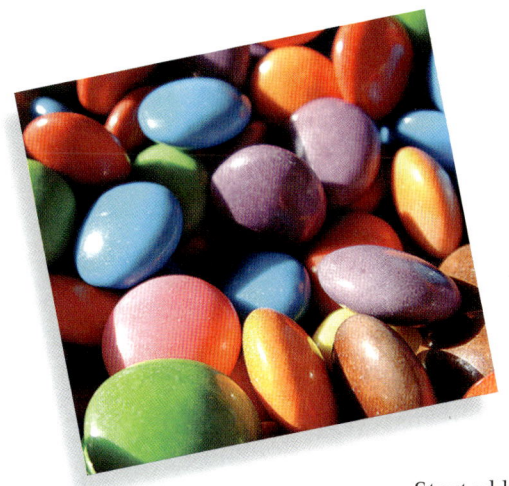

Smartie Tubes

We usually think of acorns and oak trees. But the magic of Smartie tubes lets us see pennies grow into many thousands of pounds. Started by Joy Powell and Joan Williams in 1985, The Smartie tube initiative is a great example of a fundraising idea that is simple in conception, yet makes a valuable contribution to the Hospice's funds. Members of the public were encouraged to fill up Smartie tubes with pennies and when full, donate the tubes to Saint Michael's.

In the first 5 years of the scheme, Smartie tubes raised £6,682. Income from pennies has continued to climb over the years:

1995	£13,434
1998	£21,300
2003	£36,885
2007	£51,830

Fundraising Groups

Originally known as 'support groups', in recent years they have been referred to as 'fundraising groups' to reflect more accurately their hard work and impressive fundraising achievements. Saint Michael's has always had active fundraising groups in the districts served by the charity; however, the groups and their members have changed over the years. Fundraising groups organise events, which raises valuable funds, and just as importantly, increases awareness of Saint Michael's services. The first group was 'Harrogate Support Group' – formed 25 years ago – and was involved in the very beginning of the Saint Michael's story. The most recently formed group 'Crimple Valley Fundraising Group' was established in 2011. Fundraising events organised by groups include coffee mornings, fashion shows, carol concerts, music evenings and open gardens. If you can think of it some Group is doing it!

The Harrogate Support Group

From April 2010 Saint Michael's magazine:

When and why was the group established? A group of around 25 ladies from Harrogate joined forces in response to calls from the local community for Harrogate's own palliative care service. The group of volunteers worked tirelessly to raise both awareness and funds in the local area. After Saint Michael's was granted charitable status in 1987, the group was instrumental in securing a room within Oatlands Drive Convent, for a drop-in facility and telephone. Today, 25 years on, many of the founding members of this group are still actively fundraising for Saint Michael's. The group continues to organise a coffee morning at Saint Michael's on the first Thursday of each month.

Members of the Harrogate Support Group enjoy their regular coffee morning fundraiser. Saint Michael's Magazine, April 2010

Hampsthwaite Support Group's annual Savoury Supper event at Harrogate Ladies College. After enjoying a glass of wine and 'all you can eat' supper, supporters are enjoying some entertainment provided by Harrogate Ladies College Choir, 2004

Hampsthwaite Support Group was also very active. Their Savoury Supper, with entertainment by the talented Harrogate Ladies College Chapel Choir, was a great hit every year, raising £1500 annually. Their plant stall at the annual Gala was always a big success.

Spofforth, Pateley Bridge, Masham Support Groups, too, worked hard throughout the years, with Coffee Mornings, raffles and tombolas, Spring Fairs & Galas.

Fountains and Ripon Support Groups are tirelessly dedicated in their work for Saint Michael's, regularly organising sucessful fundraising events within their communities.

Spring Fling & Christmas at Crimple

The Spring Fling (above) and Christmas at Crimple (below), run by the Harrogate Support group, were highly successful ventures, always well attended.

Planning an Event

Members of the Ripon Support Group running a cake stall in Ripon Market Square

Current members of the Ripon group

Celebrating 20 Years

Members of the Fountains Support group. Saint Michael's Magazine, September 2009

Linen and Lace stall 2002

As well as the more formally constituted Support Groups, there have been many instances of individuals getting together to help in fundraising.

The sale of **Linen and Lace** was a very successful form of early fundraising. Gathering, laundering and repairing donated linens and lace items in preparation for sale was carried out by two dedicated volunteers, and was quite an operation!

The Craft Group's stall was a regular feature at events such as the Summer Gala, Christmas at Crimple and the Spring Fling.

The Craft Group as they featured in Saint Michael's May 1990 newsletter after raising money for a new dishwasher, mainly through the sales of knitted chicks during the Easter period

Members of the original craft group running a stall at Saint Michael's Summer Gala, 2004

The **Ripley Nativity** is organised annually by a group of supporters. Held on a local farm, the crowd enjoy mulled wine, mince pies and a chance to meet the farmyard animals. Local children perform a nativity and Father Christmas drops in with presents for all.

Fundraising through the years 79

Gala Day

This important annual event, formerly known as the Garden Party, was always opened by a celebrity and was very well attended. In the photo above from the 1991 Party, the opener is Richard Whiteley.

The Garden Party was held at Crimple House for the first time on 26th June, 1993. Geoffrey Smith was the opener and the local MP Robert Banks also attended. It was a great success and raised more than £3,800.

1994 was another great success, with £3,475 being raised.

In 1995 its name was changed to Gala Day and it was held, for the first time, on a Sunday – 25th June.

Harrogate Mayor, Councillor Phillip Broadbank opened the 1996 Gala, which made over

Tombola and plant sales at the 2003 Summer Gala

Emmerdale Actor Mark Charnock opening the Summer Gala, 2005

£3,300 despite the previous day's heavy rain. There were 27 stalls, Fancy Hat competitions, live music from Echo 4-2, an Irish dancing team and 'Walkies' – the Dog Agility team. The star prize in the Grand Gala draw was a weekend for two at the Mount Hotel, Scarborough.

Summer Gala, 2003

Summer Gala, 2007

Fundraising through the years

Collection Boxes

Saint Michael's volunteer Allan Taylor is responsible for the many hundreds of collection boxes found on the counter of shops, restaurants and businesses throughout the local area. After carrying out this role for over 18 years, Allan has raised a phenomenal amount of money; after 2011's total is added, the total figure raised over the years is expected to be more than £200,000!

"When I first started there were approximately 100 boxes, mostly in Harrogate, and now I have managed to increase the number to over 500. We started with the old red barrel boxes, but I introduced the new blue ones, with a chain attached. The main thing I have done is to increase the area covered by boxes. Now we have them from Otley in the south to Masham in the north, mostly still in Harrogate, but with an increasing number in smaller villages. I spend one day per week travelling around the area to empty boxes, and to try to place new ones where I see an empty counter. Boxes can be found in shops, garages, supermarkets, pubs, tearooms and local businesses. When I started there were only about six other charities who were in competition with us, but now there are over sixty, and many of those are national charities. I keep a record of all the boxes, and of how often they need to be opened or emptied. Some are done every week, some fortnightly, and some monthly or even three-monthly. I have also instigated a gold, silver and bronze award to our top collectors each year.

These collections are really all about small change; often the coppers you receive in your change at the shop. But although we don't get cheques in our boxes, sometimes we have more than we expect; the box feels light, but I find £5 and £10 notes in it. It is an impulse to donate into a collection box, so I can find a heavy box, full of coppers, or a light box, with notes in it. On average, in 2008 a box contained £39 for the year. In 2009 it went up to £49, and in 2010 it was £53. When I started to do this 18 years ago, the boxes brought in £6,000 per annum, but last year the grand total was £20,000."

Saint Michael's shop on Cold Bath Road, with 'Yellow Month' window display, 2001

Yellow Month

> Yellow Day Ideas:
> Custard pie your boss or teacher... Have a 'Yellow Lunch'...
> Hold a Yellow raffle... Have a Yellow Saint Michael's Window Display...

Advert for 'Yellow Day', taken from Saint Michael's Spring 2001 Newsletter

June is National Hospice Awareness Month, commonly known as 'Yellow Month'. Businesses and organisations all over the UK raise thousands of pounds to help their local hospices by holding yellow themed events.

In 2004 Saint Michael's Yellow Day became Yellow Week. In more recent years this became 'Yellow Month'. Throughout June, the fundraising team is busy promoting the initiative and encouraging members of the public to get creative with their own fundraising ideas.

Saint Michael's employees sampling special edition 'Sunflower Biscuits' created by Thomas of York bakers in 2004

Yellow week (then month) has always been a popular way for local schools to support the charity. Many will hold a 'Yellow Day'; encouraging the children to wear yellow in return for a small donation, or organising fundraising events, such as the 'Yellow Day Car Wash' seen advertised here, June 2003.

Dolly Daisy was a regular participant during yellow week. Here she is with Saint Michael's employees preparing to set off around Harrogate to raise awareness of yellow week (below left), and at a local supermarket, encouraging staff and customers to 'Get Mellow, Wear Yellow' for Saint Michael's! (below right), 2007.

Saint Michael's lottery was launched to great fanfare (and a menagerie of staff members!), in Harrogate town centre, Saturday 8th April, 2000.

Saint Michael's Lottery

Launched in 2000, the lottery soon became an important and reliable source of income. Lottery members pay £1 per week to enter the draw and there are 32 chances to win, including a top prize of £1000.

The first official draw was held on 2nd June, 2000, and within a year Saint Michael's had signed up over 3,000 members. By 2004 the lottery had made over £100,000 profit. David Archbold, Regular Giving Manager, joined Saint Michael's in 2002 and has seen the lottery continue to grow:

> "Despite a fluctuating economic climate there was steady growth in the following years and 2007 saw the total membership reach 4,500. In 2009 there was a strategic campaign to ask Lottery members who were tax payers to convert from Lottery membership to Regular Giving donations, thus providing, at least, an extra 25% revenue in Gift Aid. (We cannot claim Gift Aid on Lottery subscriptions.) This reduced the numbers in the Lottery – and thereby increased the chances of winning! There followed a huge effort to attract new Lottery members and numbers continue to increase. The Lottery continues to provide vital income with an annual profit in excess of 'six figures' proving that it continues to be one of the easiest ways for individuals and 'syndicates' to support Saint Michael's."

The Engage Mutual Midnight Walk

One Night, One cause, One Community

Each summer, hundreds of Saint Michael's supporters take to the streets of Harrogate in the small hours of the morning to raise money for the charity. The 6.5 mile sponsored event attracts families, teams of colleagues and groups of friends, and the lively atmosphere and collaborative spirit is key to the event's success.

The event has grown each year and over 1000 people took part in 2011. Raising over £100,000, it is one of Saint Michael's most successful fundraising events.

Saint Michael's staff volunteering at the 2011 event

Dolly Daisy leads participants in a warm-up before Saint Michael's first 'Engage Mutual Midnight Walk', July 2007

Over 1100 people took part in the 2010 event

Fundraising through the years

Summer Ball

SAINT MICHAEL'S HOSPICE
Sunflower Ball
Friday 11 June 2004
At The Majestic Hotel, Harrogate

Champagne Reception, Music by The Spa Quartet, The NightJars and Audio Events Ltd Tree of Life, Formula One Simulator

Tickets £60 - almost sold out...... HURRY! for invitations or tickets telephone 01423 878192

A BLACK TIE EVENT NOT TO BE MISSED

This has been known by different names, including the 'Daisy Chain Ball' and the 'Sunflower Ball'. Now held biennially, the Saint Michael's black tie event remains a big hitter on the fundraising calendar.

The tables are set for the 'fire and ice' themed 2010 event

saint michael's

Unusual, Obscure and Downright Barmy!

The Duck Race

This event, held on New Year's Day, is organised by supporters of Saint Michael's who, for many years, donated the proceeds to the hospice. The sight of 5000 yellow ducks being tipped into the River Nidd is not one easily forgotten! On a number of occasions 'slow starters' were helped along by jets of water from Knaresborough's fire department's hoses!

Yellow ducks 'racing' along the River Nidd, Knaresborough, 2003

The Bed Race

Saint Michael's team drag themselves through the river shortly before the end of the gruelling course during the 2006 'Great Knaresborough Bed Race'

Coming up to its 47th year in 2012, The **'Great Knaresborough Bed Race'** has become a nationally famous event. During this unique event teams of six race a bed through the town and river. Organised by the Knaresborough Lions, participating teams raise money through sponsorship and donate to a charity of their choice. Historically, Saint Michael's has benefited from a number of teams running on behalf of the organisation; raising substantial funds. Saint Michael's also cheers along a staff team each year.

'Boxing Day Tug-of-War'

Another event that utilises the beautiful setting of the River Nidd in Knaresborough, is the **'Boxing Day Tug-of-War'**. Dating back to 1967, the competition was traditionally held between two teams from the Half Moon and Mother Shipton's pubs but in 2009 it was opened up to other local teams. Saint Michael's volunteers can be found at the event, collecting donations from a generous, festive crowd!

Tug-of war across the River Nidd, 2003

Three-legged, fancy-dress pancake day race!

Taking place in the grounds of Crimple House, this event brought together fancy dress, racing and pancake tossing (together with umbrella holding when the weather demanded it – as seen in this photograph of the 2004 event!).

Going the extra mile for Saint Michael's

Whether you are a beginner runner looking for somewhere to start, or someone looking for a once-in-a-lifetime challenge, Rob Shuker, Saint Michael's Challenge Fundraiser aims to offer something for everyone.

After joining the organisation in 2011, Rob is responsible for developing, leading and managing the growing programme of fundraising sports and activity based challenge events at Saint Michael's.

> "Whether you are trekking in Peru, or cycling the coast to coast; climbing the 3 peaks or walking the Great Wall of China, our challenge events guarantee our participants have an incredible physical challenge they will never forget and we are there for them every step of the way."

In 2011 a group of Saint Michael's supporters stepped up to the challenge of a ten day trek through Peru, taking in the 15th Century Inca site, Machu Picchu, and raising over £60,000 for the organisation.

Shops

Enterprise

Saint Michael's is well known throughout the Harrogate and surrounding districts for its well stocked and expertly run shops. The story of Saint Michael's retail fundraising begins in 1989, when Company Secretary, Dennis Holman, spotted a valuable fundraising opportunity. Pat Jackson volunteered during these early days and remains an active retail volunteer today:

> "I had worked in retail for many years and ran my own business so Dennis Holman took me under his wing and we formed the Harrogate District Hospice Care Enterprises Ltd.

> "We set it up as a Limited Company, registered with Companies House, and each paid £1 to open the account. Dennis was wonderful, he encouraged me so much, and when he died in 1992 I was asked to take over the business as buyer for the Enterprises. The idea was that we would have a stock of goods and gifts which we would sell at local events. Muriel Little would give a talk and a slide show about what the hospice was all about and answer people's questions, and I

Pat Jackson setting up a stall at a Saint Michael's Summer Gala, 1992

would run the stall, selling everything; tea-towels, packs of note-lets, Christmas cards, calendars.

"The most important thing was our logo – everything was marked with Saint Michael's Hospice so that the people of Harrogate area would recognize that what they were buying was directly supporting their Hospice. The stalls were really popular – we went to craft fairs, WI meetings, coffee mornings.

"The Enterprise ran from 1989–1999 and created a lot of income throughout the year. At Christmas our cards and calendars went all over the world. We were accountable to the Company Secretary for everything, so we bought in comparatively small amounts – it was a case of money out before money in, and we didn't want to be left holding a lot of stock we couldn't sell. The staff at the hospice and the day patients were all good customers too!"

Above and right: Volunteers working hard to raise valuable funds through the sale of enterprise goods in the grounds of Crimple House

Volunteer Muriel Little (second from left) and fellow volunteers running a Saint Michael's temporary shop in the Lowther Arcade, Cambridge Street, Harrogate, December 1991

Temporary Shops

In the run up to Christmas 1991, Saint Michael's supporters and volunteers worked constantly to secure events and locations at which to sell their growing selection of Enterprise goods. A stroke of luck came when the old Leamington Spa Building Society premises, in Cambridge Street, Harrogate, became vacant, and a band of volunteers took the opportunity to open a temporary shop. Setting up in just one day, the volunteers worked tirelessly throughout November and December. **The final profit was an unbelievable £12,000.**

This was the beginning of Retail Fundraising for Saint Michael's. The group immediately began to look for a permanent shop they could take on. It was to be some time, but their persistence was rewarded late the following year, with the opening of the very first Saint Michael's charity shop.

Since then Saint Michael's has gone on to open eight more shops, and retail fundraising remains one of the most reliable and important sources of income for the charity.

Cold Bath Road

Opened November 1992
In November 1992 Saint Michael's retail team moved into an empty shop on Cold Bath Road, Harrogate. As in previous years, this was intended to be a temporary pop-up shop. However, this venture

proved so successful that the need for a permanent shop became ever more clear. Pat Jackson became the volunteer manager of Saint Michael's shop on Cold Bath Road when it opened in November 1992:

"We opened our first shop in Cold Bath Road in November 1992, and to begin with we just sold the Enterprise goods – it was over the Christmas period and we had a very successful time. As a result, we went to the Council of Management of the Hospice and suggested that we could use the same premises to open as an ordinary Charity Shop, and they agreed.

Celebrating the Queen's Golden Jubilee in 2002

Volunteer Catherine Winter and Brenda Exall celebrating the re-opening of the shop after substantial refurbishment in June 2004

"We opened on 1 October 1993, selling a combination of donated items and Enterprise goods. We were able to get some good publicity through the newsletter and the local papers, and donated goods started to pour in. We knew that many of our items came as a result of bereavement – the people who had been nursed in the hospice would often specify that their clothes, books etc should be given to the shop, and we **always** accepted everything."

Leeds Road

Opened Summer 1994
A couple of years after the opening of the shop on Cold Bath Road, an opportunity arose to open a second shop, which the Chairman of Saint Michael's was quick to seize, as Volunteer Pat Jackson remembers:

"I remember the chairman Wyn Davies asking me, at the outset, 'How much do you think these shops might raise?' and I replied that I would be very disappointed if we didn't take £100 per day. Of course, like Topsy, the whole project just grew and we soon opened the Leeds Road shop, with me in charge."

Saint Michael's shop on Leeds Road is currently managed by volunteer Muriel Little; she recalls some memorable donations:

"I really enjoyed the adult-sized Pink Rabbit outfit – I wonder where it had been used before?! We have also had some valuable items of jewellery, and very high quality items. One of the most memorable was a Tibetan national costume. We are so lucky that we have a really good relationship with a local auctioneers, who will value anything for us free of charge and put it into the auction without cost. They have been really generous supporters."

Bilton shop is re-opened after refurbishment, by Emmerdale Actor Mark Charnock on 10th August 2005

Bilton

Opened in 1998

Saint Michael's third shop was opened in the Bilton area of Harrogate in October 1998. It proved an exciting new venture and although spacious, it became clear that more room was required. Donations from the local community came in with great enthusiasm and the volunteers were soon over-run by black bags full of potential treasures. Fortunately, the flat directly above the shop became available soon after the Saint Michael's team moved in and they jumped at the opportunity to use this additional space, which provided room to sort and price donated goods. The shop remains very successful today.

Retail volunteer, Pat Jackson, remembers how the additional work that this third shop required affected her volunteer role:

> "With three shops up and running, it was a real case of good teamwork. Originally I did all the cashing up, and kept the money in my house! Of course all that has changed now, thank goodness, and it is collected professionally."

Starbeck

Opened 7th December 2004

After pausing for breath for a few years, Saint Michael's retail team, under the guidance of a new Chief Executive, Graham Archer, expanded further, opening a shop in the Starbeck area of Harrogate. On this occasion a celebrity endorsement really got the public excited.

Actor Hugo Speer enjoys a cuddle with Dolly Daisy at the official opening of Saint Michael's Starbeck shop, December 2007

The newly refurbished shop in 2010

Cold Bath Road Furniture Shop

Opened July 2007

In an exciting new venture, Saint Michael's opened a dedicated second hand furniture shop, close to the original shop on Cold Bath Road, Harrogate in the summer of 2007

Otley

Opened December 2007

Saint Michael's reaches a wide catchment area with its services. In 2007 this was reflected in the opening of a new shop in Otley.

Community support was superb and in an exciting development in 2010, the shop was re-launched as a dedicated second hand bookshop.

Even driving rain couldn't keep Dolly Daisy away from the official opening of Saint Michael's Otley shop, December 2007

Customers poured into the newly opened shop, showing their support from the outset

Members of Harrogate College's joinery department donated their skills and time and created beautiful custom fit shelves

Retail volunteers visiting the shop shortly before its official re-launch in July 2010

Knaresborough

Opened December 2007
In what proved to be an extremely busy year for Saint Michael's retail team, Knaresborough was the location of the fourth shop to open during 2007.

In 2010 Saint Michael's shop in Knaresborough was refurbished. Pictured are current Manager Linda Denovan (far left) and three members of her volunteer team

Ripon

Opened January 2008

The opening of a shop in Ripon in January 2008 helped to strengthen links with the local community, increasing awareness of Saint Michael's services. It also bolstered already thriving fundraising for Saint Michael's in the area.

The retail team was relieved when the shop in Ripon finally opened its door to the public, as they had been looking for suitable premises in the area for over three years!

Jennyfield

Opened October 2010

The Saint Michael's shop in the Jennyfield area of Harrogate is the most recent addition and is already thriving. The precedent for hard work and sound business plans set by a small group of volunteers over twenty years ago remains, and, from a temporary shop to nine thriving shops, they have quite a legacy to look back on!

A former hairdressing salon in the Jennyfield area of Harrogate is transformed into Saint Michael's latest shop

Retail Volunteers

Volunteers have always been pivotal to the success of retail fundraising at Saint Michael's. In the early days of Enterprise goods and temporary shops, volunteers alone carried out the buying, selling and everything in between. Indeed the Saint Michael's shops remained managed by volunteers until 2007, when, in keeping with charity shops across the country, paid managers were introduced. Today these managers are supported by almost four hundred volunteers, dedicated and hard working individuals who sort items, price, sell, smile, chat, and continue to be the very heart of the shops.

A volunteer since Saint Michael's conception, Muriel Little (far right) remains the only volunteer shop manager

Retail volunteers are the organisation's representatives in the community and offer a far-reaching connection with the public.

Saint Michael's pop-up shop, Parliament Street, Harrogate, July 2011

Pop-Up Shops

'Pop-up' shops provided Saint Michael's with its very first foray into retailing, over twenty years ago (then termed 'temporary shops'), and have returned with a flourish in recent years. Having prepared thoroughly, the Saint Michael's retail team can now take over a vacant shop within a day, offering a professionally run retail store, regardless of whether the vacant store is available for two days, one week or several months. Amanda Wilson, Saint Michael's Retail Manager was involved in a recent pop up shop:

> "Customers shopped with us without realising we were a charity shop. We challenged people's expectations and attracted new types of customer. More importantly, we raised a lot of money in a short space of time."

Online Selling

Online selling is becoming increasingly common and in 2010 Saint Michael's began using this method. Specialist items are identified in the shops and brought to a central location where they are carefully photographed and described before being listed for sale on various websites. This opens the organization up to a global market which has proved to be very successful. The Saint Michael's eBay fundraiser recounts an unusual sale:

> "One of our most interesting items was a World War One Royal Fleet Artillery Jacket with 3 pairs of matching trousers. It was donated to the Jennyfields shop by a man whose grandfather had owned it. It was very moth eaten and crumbling but it was an interesting piece of history. It sold on eBay for £835. It realized this price because it was a rare piece of world war one uniform, and hardly any survive. The man was very pleased about the amount raised and that it all was going towards Saint Michaels. We get many items donated to our charity shops that are worth over £100 every week, and a lot of the time these can be missed in the shops because there are so many niche markets on eBay that most people don't know about. This is most likely because the market is open to all over the world. We have sold items to countries as far as Australia, Qatar, China, Japan, Brazil and Canada."

Recycling

Saint Michael's has always promoted recycling within its shops. By their very nature, Charity shops are a form of recycling; goods donated to shops might otherwise have ended up in landfill. Saint Michael's sells as many donated items as possible, and those that are not in a saleable condition are recycled wherever possible. Recycling in this way actually raises money, adding to the overall profitability of retail fundraising. Nearly all items can be recycled effectively, from mobile phones and foreign coins to electrical goods, books and textiles.

Volunteers at Saint Michael's

Saint Michael's was, as we have seen, founded by a small group of volunteers. By 1993 this had grown to approximately eighty volunteers. Their main tasks included cooking, cleaning, driving patients to and from Day Care, running the shops and fundraising.

By 1997 there were almost three hundred volunteers. This increase was largely due to additional shops opening, each requiring up to thirty volunteers. Services had expanded, requiring additional volunteer support, and increasing running costs demanded much of Saint Michael's numerous fundraising volunteers.

Volunteers were invited to accept long-service awards in 2001. Many were involved in the very beginnings of Saint Michael's. And many continue as volunteers in 2011!

By 2011 six hundred volunteers were involved in the work of Saint Michael's carrying out over fifty different roles. Miriam Landy, Volunteer Co-ordinator at Saint Michael's explains further:

> "We are in an unusual situation at Saint Michael's as we need to carry out very little advertising to attract volunteers. We are so well supported by our local communities that new volunteers are applying all the time; I receive around four enquiries each week. That's not to say that we don't welcome additional help! There's always more to be done and volunteers are now involved in increasingly varied roles. We have an 'Equal Opportunities Analysis' volunteer, a number of 'Legacy Champion' volunteers and a whole host of other roles that really make the best use of the considerable skills and experience of those who want to help. The nature of volunteering is also changing – volunteers are often looking for a temporary role, perhaps for only a couple of weeks. Others would like to become a 'full time' volunteer for six weeks to get some great experience for their CV. We have learnt to be very flexible in our approach to involving volunteers and the rewards have been plentiful"

Christine Upton began volunteering in 2007, supporting the inpatient unit. She is pictured preparing the trolley for an afternoon tea service offered to patients and visitors. Christine is also Saint Michael's volunteer writer-in-residence, contributing every three months to the publication of a newsletter for volunteers

Sandra Gilbert signed up as a volunteer in 2008 and like Christine, she also multi-tasks. Sandra juggles helping in one of Saint Michael's shops with co-ordinating Saint Michael's most recently formed Fundraising Group

Merlin Fozard joined Saint Michael's Day Therapy team as a volunteer in 2004. He spends each Tuesday at Saint Michael's, offering support to patients and practical help to the Day Therapy team

Isobel Beard has been serving afternoon tea to patients and visitors at Saint Michael's since 2002. Saint Michael's has many such long serving volunteers: In 2011, 106 of Saint Michael's 620 volunteers have been helping for ten years or more

Volunteers at saint michael's

Jo Walker became a volunteer receptionist at Saint Michael's in 2010. Jo, and her fellow reception volunteers, represent the first impression of Saint Michael's for many patients, visitors and telephone callers

Leonard Hulme is a gardening volunteer and joined the organisation in 2010. He is also a member of Saint Michael's Volunteer Advisory Group and meets with Tony Collins, Chief Executive of Saint Michael's, every three months to discuss the management of the organisation and plans for the future

Some volunteers join Saint Michael's only briefly, each making their mark and then moving on. For others Saint Michael's has been an integral part of their lives over many years. Glenys Davies was present at the inaugural meeting of the Wheatfields Hospice Harrogate Support group in 1977, was an active volunteer throughout the creation and development of Saint Michael's and, thirty four years later, continues as a retail volunteer today. Her husband Wynn Davies played a vital role in the early governance of the organisation as Chairman of the Council of Management between 1994 and 2000.

Wynn pictured in the grounds of Crimple House, shortly before his retirement in 2000

Glenys in 2001, after receiving a volunteer long-service award

Like many of Saint Michael's volunteers, Julie Dunlop became a volunteer after a personal experience of Saint Michael's services:

"It will be 21 years this Christmas that I became involved. When my husband was diagnosed with cancer the hospice was just being talked about – he died in July 1987. At the end of 1988 my aunt, who lived in a flat in Harrogate, was diagnosed with cancer. She came to live with me, but her doctor suggested that she should go into Saint Michael's to give me a break – just for a week. Unfortunately she was very, very ill, and she never came home again – she died on 26 November that year.

"After the funeral, I went in to the Hospice the following week to thank everyone for what they had done, and I asked if there was anything I could do to help. They immediately suggested that they could really do with someone to cook the meal on Saturday evening. This was at Oatlands, when the cooking was done by volunteers. So I agreed, and I did that for four years."

Julie Dunlop, Saint Michael's volunteer, 1990 - present

Julie went on to volunteer on Saint Michael's inpatient unit, supporting the nursing staff by carrying out a whole variety of administrative and practical tasks. Although ultimately very rewarding, volunteering on the inpatient unit is not without its challenges, as Julie explains:

"It is never depressing, although sometimes it is very upsetting. At that point, when you leave, you must say to yourself 'I can't do any more today, I have done what I can, and I have done it to the best of my ability, and when I go in next week, I can do it again.'

"The doctors, nurses and health care assistants do the most amazing job, and they are so grateful for everything that the volunteers do. They treat us as friends and colleagues, and that makes me feel wanted – it has all been a very positive experience."

The 'Saint Michael's Effect'

"The 'Saint Michael's Effect' comes from the people who work here – it is all about the values of positivity, of living lives to the full, and of treating each and every person as an individual." *Tony Collins, Saint Michael's Chief Executive, 2011*

"The nursing staff stay because they love the job: it's real nursing. They do have to have a lot of training – nowadays hospice nursing is included in nurse training but it wasn't before. I remember thinking what a happy place it was and how privileged I was to work there – in a way, it was like being a midwife, and I was honoured to be there at people's goings as a midwife would be at their births." *Ursula Darley, Nursing Sister, 1990*

"I have no experience of Saint Michael's Hospice being 'a place where people die'. It's a place where you live. The attitude of the staff is so positive and encouraging that it does your soul and spirits good just to be there. They are an excellent group, and the expansion of services is just as it ought to be. The attraction of the Hospice is not just the brilliant team there. It is in the building itself – the setting is fabulous. When I was working, I would sometimes drive up there; not to see a patient, but just to sit in the garden for a bit of peace and quiet. I could sum up Saint Michael's with just one word: 'Compassion' – it just oozes out of the place." *Dr Bob Jones, Harrogate GP*

"Once you come to work at the Hospice, you never want to work anywhere else. Of course some people did move on, because they moved or for some family reason, and sadly some of the staff have died in the Hospice. It's a wonderful community, and made me feel very humble to be part of it. There is a real family feeling of closeness, everybody cares for everybody else – because of course the staff need care too. There is always somebody who pulls at your heartstrings for whom you go the extra mile. And sometimes it's the patients who gee you up and you get strength from them – if they can smile then you can!

"I've never been afraid of dying, but like everyone else I have had questions. But once you see the look on someone's face of such serenity – in fact, I've seen one patient who had the look of expectation of what was to follow – you understand what dying in a Hospice means." *Pauline Wiggins, Housekeeper and Volunteer Organiser, 1990*

"My abiding memory of Saint Michael's is one of enjoyment firstly. I have really enjoyed all that I have achieved, and I have a huge amount of satisfaction from the hard work I have done and in the good and lasting friendships I have made.

"The main thing is that when it started, the Hospice was like an old fashioned cottage hospital, but it grew day by day, and its reputation grew, but it is still Harrogate's **own** Hospice. Local people still want to give their 50ps, or £1s, to support it.

"I think, it's a place where you are accepted, a place of peace, and also a place where you are always learning from the other people you meet there." *Pat Jackson, Saint Michael's Volunteer, 1990 – present*

"It's a wonderful place and a real privilege to work there. It's really what nursing is all about; nursing the patients and their families together. Nothing should be too much trouble. It's also a place of honesty. Patients have lots of questions, sometimes about their care, sometimes about more ordinary things. We had the time to explain everything, honestly, but with love – that's what it is all about. People only have a short time left, and they want to be at peace. When a lady dies, we always used to put a flower by her head – we had the time and the love and the care to do that so that when her family came to say goodbye, she looked beautiful. They don't remember the tubes and stuff, they remember her being peaceful and asleep.

"The hospice is a building that is not a building; it's a place full of love, kindness, care and hope; it's not bricks and mortar – it's a living, breathing place." *Kath Gill, nursing Sister, 1990*

"The teams who deliver the care and support within all aspects of the work of Saint Michael's do so with unfailing commitment, devotion and professionalism. The sheer skill, attention to detail and expertise is evident throughout. Our reason for working at Saint Michael's is founded on the very strong desire to make a tangible difference to enhance the quality of life of all who are entrusted into our care. We strive to respond to complex medical and physical conditions, delicate social and emotional pressures, deep spiritual struggles and a loss of control, identity, a need for great tenderness and the restoring of the persons whole identity.

Care of patients loved ones, support to visitors, volunteers and staff alike is offered in a warm, natural and gentle way as we travel alongside those who need our care, and caring for each other along the way. We have evolved so far in what we can offer to our community, yet as pioneers, will always want to give even more – life is too short to ever compromise the standard of care we deliver." *Ann Cairns, Director of Clinical Services, 1997–Present*